Designed and produced by
Aladdin Books Ltd
70 Old Compton Street
London W1

Design   David West
Children's Book Design
Editorial Planning   Clark Robinson Limited
Editor   Bibby Whittaker
Researcher   Cecilia Weston-Baker
Illustrated by   Ron Hayward Associates

EDITORIAL PANEL
The author Keith Lye, has worked
as an editor and lecturer on
geography in Great Britain, Africa
and the United States.

The educational consultant, Peter
Thwaites, is Head of Geography at
Windlesham House School in
Sussex.

The editorial consultant, John Clark,
has contributed to many
information and reference books.

*First published in the
United States in 1987 by*
Gloucester Press
387 Park Avenue South
New York, NY 10016

ISBN 0-531-17068-3

Library of Congress Catalog
Card Number: 87-80454

Printed in Belgium

TODAY'S WORLD

EUROPE

KEITH LYE

Consultant Editor

GLOUCESTER PRESS
New York · London · Toronto · Sydney

CONTENTS

How the maps work

This book has two main kinds of maps. The physical map on pages 4 and 5, shows what the land is like – indicating rivers (blue lines), mountain ranges (purple and dark brown), forests (dark green) and deserts (beige).

The red lines on the physical map divide the regions which are dealt with in the individual chapters. Therefore, the shape of a region on the physical map corresponds to the shape of the region's political map.

The political maps, such as that on page 8, show the boundaries and names of all the countries in a region. Black squares indicate the location of the capital cities. Arranged around the maps are the flags of each country, together with the type of government, name of the capital city, population and land area.

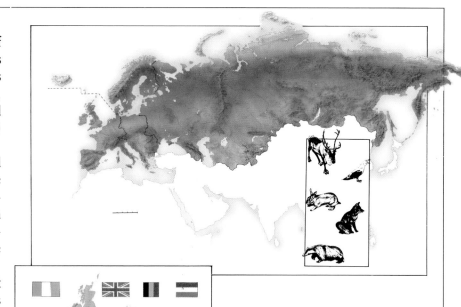

Animal panel

Alongside the physical map on page 4 is an illustrated panel of animals which can be found in Europe. Beneath each picture is the animal's common name and Latin name.

INTRODUCTION

This book is about Europe, which has four distinct parts. These are *Western Europe*, *Northern Europe*, the combination of *Central and Eastern Europe*, and the huge expanse of the *Soviet Union* (USSR). The USSR is included within this book because most of its population lives in the European part of the country, although about three-quarters of the USSR lies east of the Ural Mountains in Asia.

Europe is the most highly industrialized region of the world and contains rich, developed countries. One of the ways experts measure a country's wealth is by its per capita gross national product (GNP). This is the total value of all goods and services produced by a country divided by its number of inhabitants. Per capita GNP figures for Europe in 1984 ranged from US$900 for Albania to $15,990 for Switzerland. These figures contrast with India, a developing country, whose per capita GNP in the same year was only $260.

Europe is also a region of great diversity, containing 33 countries, including the USSR. There are more than 150 ethnic or national groups, speaking more than 50 different languages.

The Eiffel Tower has dominated the skyline of Paris since it was completed in 1889

Area (Europe and the USSR):
27,195,612 sq km
(10,500,225 sq miles).
Highest peak
Mount Elbrus, 5,642 m
(18,510 ft) in European USSR
Communism Peak, 7,495 m
(24,590 ft) in Asian USSR
Lowest point on land
(USSR): Karagiye Depression
by the Caspian Sea, 132 m
(433 ft) below sea level.
Longest river
Volga, 3,690 km (2,293 miles)
in European USSR;
Yenisey, 5,539 km
(3,442 miles) in Asian USSR.

Part of Europe lies north within the Arctic Circle. Northern Europe is mainly mountainous, while Western, Central and Eastern Europe are dominated by the uplands that stretch from the Pyrénées through the Alps to the Carpathian Mountains. To the west and north of these uplands is a wide, fertile crescent of low-lying agricultural land known as the North European Plain. To the east the Ural Mountains divide the rolling landscape of the European USSR from the Siberian Plain in Asia. Vast coniferous forests cover much of Northern Europe and the Soviet Union. These give way to temperate forests further south.

Herring gull
Larus argentatus

Reindeer
Rangifer tarandus

Rabbit
Oryctolagus cuniculus

Fox
Vulpes vulpes

Badger
Meles taxus

Arctic Circle

Novaya Zemlya
KARA SEA
BARENTS SEA
NORWEGIAN SEA
Northwest mountains
NORTHERN EUROPE
WHITE SEA
Pechora
Lake Ladoga
Lake Onega
N. Dvina
Plain
Urals
Valdai Hills
European
Central Russian Uplands
EUROPE
BALTIC SEA
NORTH SEA
Dvina
Dnepr
Don
Volga
Ural-Caspian Lowlands
Rhine
North
Elbe
Carpathians
Dnestr
WESTERN EUROPE
Massif Central
Alps
Dinaric Alps
Danube
Elbrus ▲
Caucasus
CASPIAN SEA
ARAL SEA
Pyrénées
Apennines
BLACK SEA
Kyzylku desert
Meseta
Balkan Mountains
MEDITERRANEAN SEA
CENTRAL AND EASTERN EUROPE

SCALE

0   200   400 Miles

0   400   800 Kilometers

Varied climate

While Northern Europe has long, cold winters and short summers, the Mediterranean countries of Western Europe have hot, dry summers and mild, wet winters. Further east, winters become cooler. In the southeastern USSR there are steppe (grassland) regions with great changes in daily temperature and little rainfall. Most of Europe receives about 50-150 cm (20-60 inches) of rain each year. Mountain regions in the west, including parts of Norway and the United Kingdom, receive 200 cm (80 inches) of rainfall annually. Regions to the east of mountains get much less rain.

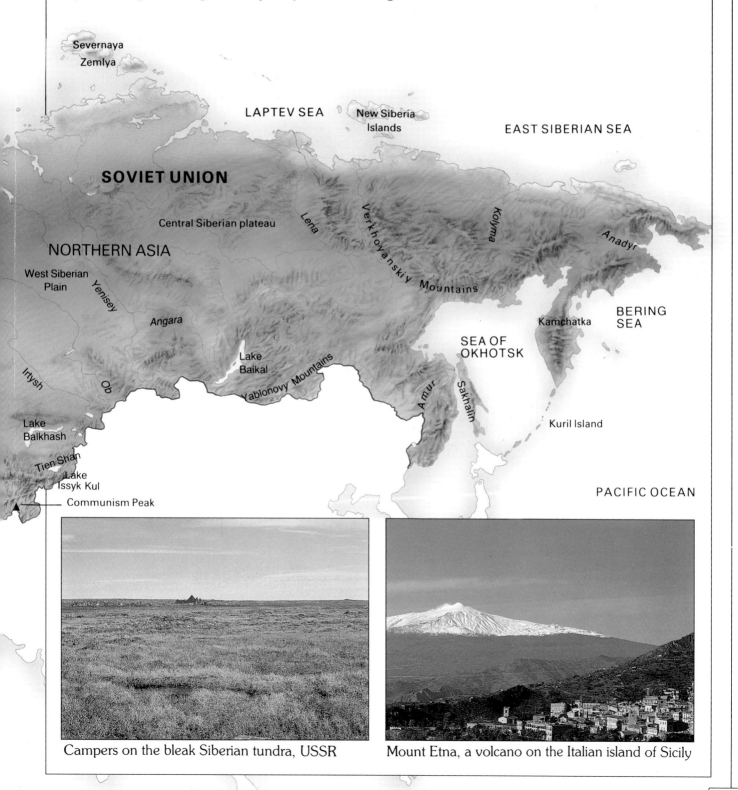

Severnaya Zemlya

LAPTEV SEA

New Siberia Islands

EAST SIBERIAN SEA

SOVIET UNION

Central Siberian plateau

Lena

Verkhoyanskiy Mountains

Kolyma

Anadyr

NORTHERN ASIA

West Siberian Plain

Yenisey

Angara

BERING SEA

Kamchatka

SEA OF OKHOTSK

Lake Baikal

Yablonovy Mountains

Irtysh

Ob

Amur

Sakhalin

Kuril Island

Lake Balkhash

Tien Shan

Lake Issyk Kul

Communism Peak

PACIFIC OCEAN

Campers on the bleak Siberian tundra, USSR

Mount Etna, a volcano on the Italian island of Sicily

5

EUROPEAN PEOPLES

Population: (Europe and USSR): 772,927,000.
Population density:
72 per sq km (187 per sq mile).
Largest cities:
Paris France: 10,073,000
Moscow USSR: 8,642,000
London England: 6,776,000
Leningrad USSR: 4,867,000

Europe has more people than any other continent except Asia, and accounts for 16 per cent of the world's population. The USSR has the highest population with 280 million people; the Vatican City State has the lowest with only 737 in 1986. The majority of the people in Europe live in urban areas.

In some countries farming is mechanized with large areas of agricultural land farmed by only a few people. However, fruit growing, dairy farming and various other traditional small-scale agricultural enterprises throughout Europe still employ many people.

Ethnic groups

There is a wide variety of ethnic and language groups in Europe. In many cases, a country has two or more groups within its borders, and sometimes this gives rise to conflict. For example, Yugoslavia's population is made up of several groups, including the Serbs and the Croats, who have their own separate governments and a strong sense of ethnic identity. However, the Basques in northern Spain are an ethnic minority that does not have political autonomy. Groups within the Basque population have fought actively against the government in an attempt to gain greater independence.

Physical types range from the tall, blond, blue-eyed Scandinavians, to the shorter, dark-haired Mediterranean peoples of southern Spain, Italy and Greece. Many Asian and black people also live in Europe, having emigrated from parts of Asia, Africa or the Caribbean islands in search of work.

The USSR has the widest variety of physical types because its population includes both Europeans and Asians.

A Greek has typical Mediterranean features

A Scandinavian woman

Religion

Christianity dominates Europe, although other faiths, such as Judaism and Islam, also have many followers. Christians in Europe form three major groups: Roman Catholics, Protestants and Eastern Orthodox. In Eastern Europe, in the Communist countries, religion is officially discouraged. Nevertheless, in Poland church attendance is the highest in Europe and nearly 80 per cent of the population are practicing Roman Catholics.

Liverpool Cathedral, England

Languages

About 50 languages and more than 100 dialects are spoken throughout Europe. European languages fall into two families. Most of them are "Indo-European" languages, such as Russian, German, Italian and English, together with "Uralic and Altaic" languages, such as Finnish and Hungarian. One exception is the Basque language, spoken in parts of Spain and France. It is not related to any other known language.

Jeg kan taler Dansk
Danish

Puhun suomea
Finnish

Jed snakker norsk
Norwegian

Говорю по русский
Russian

Jag talar svenska
Swedish

Parlo italiano
Italian

Ich spreche deutsch
German

Μιλώ Ελληνικά
Greek

Ja govorim srpsko-hrvatski
Serbo-Croat

Ik spreek Nederlands
Dutch

Beszélek magyarul
Hungarian

I speak English
English

Je parle français
French

Hablo español
Spanish

Mówię po polsku
Polish

Ég tala islensku.
Icelandic

Ways of life

Europe is dominated by two opposing ways of life: Communism and capitalism. The Communist countries in Eastern Europe have governments that control industry, commerce and choices of jobs and homes. The governments are dominated by Communist Party members, who represent only a small percentage of the population.

In the capitalist countries the individual has freedom of choice, and the governments are elected by the people. In most of these countries the governments run the welfare services and some essential industries. In all countries unemployment has become a problem in recent years.

British voters reelected the Conservative Party in 1987

Population: 22,794,000.
Area: 1,257,484 sq km
(485,515 sq miles).
Population density: 18 per
sq km (47 per sq mile).
Economy: The gross national
product per person in 1984
was $11,809 (ranging from
$9,040 in Iceland to $12,838
in Norway), which makes this
the richest region in Europe.

Northern Europe includes the Scandinavian countries of
Denmark, Sweden and Norway along with Finland and
Iceland. Apart from the USSR it is the most thinly populated
region in Europe.

All five countries have a high standard of living. For
example, Sweden has some of the best welfare services in
the world. It also has very little illiteracy, the highest life
expectancy and the lowest infant mortality rate in the region.
Unemployment in Northern Europe averaged only 5 per cent
in 1984, which was much lower than most of the rest of Europe.

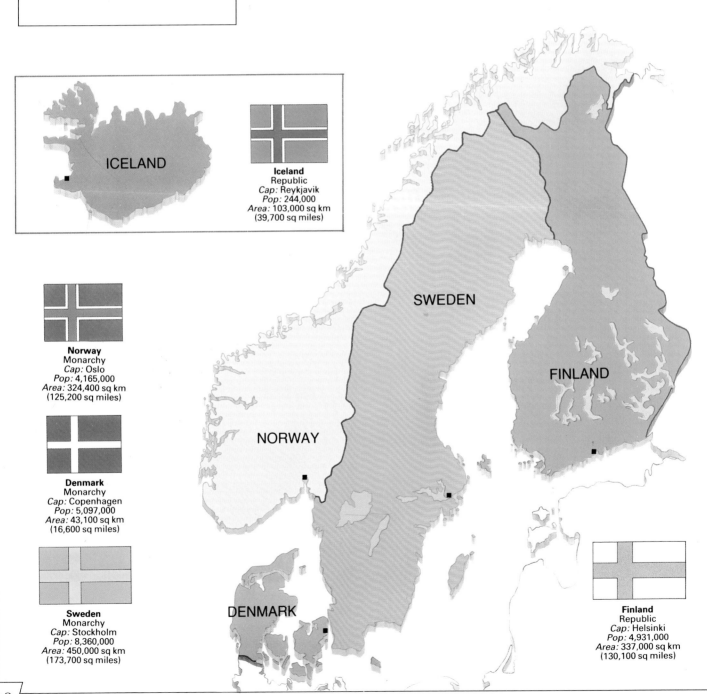

ICELAND

Iceland
Republic
Cap: Reykjavik
Pop: 244,000
Area: 103,000 sq km
(39,700 sq miles)

Norway
Monarchy
Cap: Oslo
Pop: 4,165,000
Area: 324,400 sq km
(125,200 sq miles)

Denmark
Monarchy
Cap: Copenhagen
Pop: 5,097,000
Area: 43,100 sq km
(16,600 sq miles)

Sweden
Monarchy
Cap: Stockholm
Pop: 8,360,000
Area: 450,000 sq km
(173,700 sq miles)

Finland
Republic
Cap: Helsinki
Pop: 4,931,000
Area: 337,000 sq km
(130,100 sq miles)

SWEDEN

NORWAY

FINLAND

DENMARK

Land and climate

The glacier in action

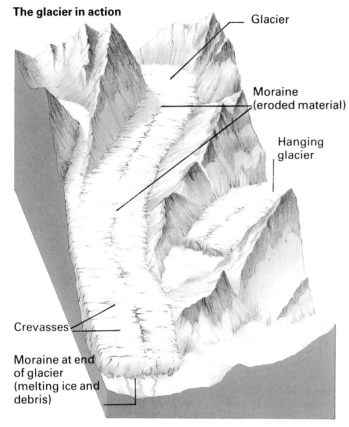

Glacier

Moraine
(eroded material)

Hanging
glacier

Crevasses

Moraine at end
of glacier
(melting ice and
debris)

The landscape of most of Northern Europe is dominated by the Northwest Mountains, which are much older than the mountains of southern Europe. They have been worn down over millions of years by the action of ice so that the highest peak, Glittertinden in Norway, is only 2,470 meters (8,104 ft) high.

The landscape has also been shaped by valley glaciers. These huge sheets of ice move down the sides of mountains under the pressure of their own weight. They erode the landscape as they go, scouring out the deep fiords and jagged coastlines of the area. The largest glacier in Europe is the Jostedal glacier in Norway, which covers a massive 780 sq km (300 sq miles). Some glaciers move very slowly, whereas others can move at a rate of up to 15 meters (50 ft) a day.

Northern Europe has a cold climate, with short, cool summers and long, cold winters. The coldest conditions prevail in the north and interior of Scandinavia and in all but the southern edge of Iceland. As a result, most of the people in this region live towards the south of each country, where the climate is warmer.

The land after glaciation

"U" shaped
valley

Debris left
by glacier

Hanging
valley

Truncated
spur

Glacial lake
(often elongated)

Waterfall

Moraine

A deep fiord in central Norway

A geyser bubbles up in Iceland

Cross-country skiing is a popular sport in Scandinavia

In common with the rest of Europe, the people in Northern Europe are urban dwellers. Nevertheless, they also place great value upon physical fitness and outdoor sports. Many children learn to ski almost as soon as they can walk. Rather than watching sports, adults are in general much more interested in participating in such sporting activities as cross-country skiing, ski-jumping, skating, walking, mountain climbing, boating and swimming. Soccer is a popular spectator sport.

Because of the cold climate and the large areas of mountainous country, crop growing is generally less important than dairy and other forms of farming. Due to the length of the coastline and the abundance of natural harbors, all the Northern European countries are renowned as nations of explorers and seafarers, and fishing is a vital industry.

Culture and the arts are particularly important to North Europeans. Figures of international renown include the Norwegian painter Edvard Munch and composer Edvard Grieg, the Finnish composer Jean Sibelius, the Danish writer Hans Christian Andersen and the Swedish filmmaker Ingmar Bergman and playwright August Strindberg.

The sauna originated in Finland

Land of the Midnight Sun

From the Arctic Circle northwards, there are times during the year when the Sun does not set even at night. There are also periods when it does not appear above the horizon. Northern Norway, Sweden and Finland are known as the "Land of the Midnight Sun" because in summer they have a period of continuous sunlight. In the winter, some parts of these countries have three months when the Sun never rises.

The phenomenon of the "Midnight Sun" occurs because the Earth's axis is tilted. In the northern summer, the North Pole leans towards the Sun. In the northern winter, the South Pole leans towards the Sun, so the North Pole has six months of darkness.

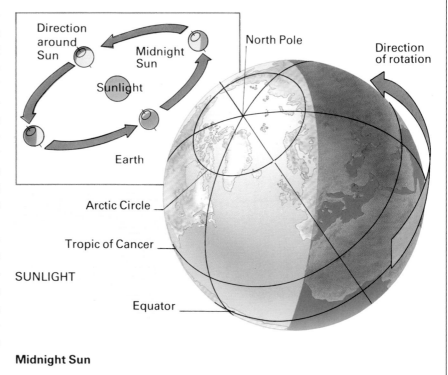

Midnight Sun

Peoples and languages

Scandinavian peoples form the great majority of the population of Northern Europe. The Danes include a small minority group of West German origin, but otherwise are all Scandinavian, with a language that is similar to Norwegian and Swedish. Iceland was originally settled by Norwegians, and the Icelandic language still has much in common with ancient Norwegian, or Old Norse. Swedish and Norwegian are both of Nordic origin and are similar.

The Finnish language, however, is unlike the Scandinavian languages and, among other European languages, it has most in common with Hungarian. Swedish is the second official language Much of the history and folklore originates from the days of the Vikings. From the 8th century these seafarers set sail in their famous Viking longboats and settled in many parts of Europe.

Discovery of Greenland by Erik the Red AD 935

Bergen, Norway, at midnight in summer

Nomadic herdsmen

Lapland covers parts of the extreme north of Norway, Sweden, Finland and the USSR. It is named after the people who live there, the Lapps. It is a cold, bleak and mostly barren land. Most Lapps are nomadic, and travel constantly with their herds of reindeer, which provide their clothing, food, transportation, and income from the sale of skins. Radioactive fallout from the nuclear accident at Chernobyl in the USSR in 1986 has contaminated the lichens on which reindeer feed, threatening the herds and the lifestyle of the Lapps. Some Lapps have settled either along the coast or beside rivers and lakes where they farm, fish and hunt for a living.

Lapland reindeer were affected by Chernobyl's radioactive fallout

Recent history

The recent history of the Northern European countries has been characterized largely by political stability and economic success. Their economies continue to expand, from a growth rate of 1.0 per cent in Sweden to 3.4 per cent in Norway in recent years. Only in Iceland is the population increasing at more than 0.4 per cent annually, so that most people in Scandinavia become wealthier each year as they benefit from an increasing share of the nation's wealth.

The only area of international conflict has been between Iceland and its neighbors in the fishing community. Iceland depends in a great part upon its fish stocks and fish products form 80% of its exports. In 1972, Iceland extended its official fishing limits

Fishing is a most important industry in Iceland

from the original 22 km (12 miles) to 93 km (50 miles). In 1975 it extended them again, this time to 370 km (200 miles), in an attempt to preserve stocks of cod. This led to several clashes in a "Cod War" between Icelandic and foreign vessels.

Giant North Sea oil platforms

Logs for the Finnish paper-making industry

The most important natural resources in Northern Europe are the softwood forests, hydroelectricity and North Sea oil. Fishing also plays a vital role in these countries' economies.

Hydroelectricity is created when water running downhill is dammed so that its energy can be harnessed to drive an electricity generator. It is a major source of power in Norway and Sweden. Iceland also has geothermal power resources from the volcanic geysers on the island.

Vast areas of Northern Europe are covered with forest, mainly coniferous, so forestry and allied industries – such as wood pulp, papermaking and timber – are important. There are also deposits of minerals such as iron ore, one of Sweden's major exports, and silver, copper and zinc, which provide the raw materials for a number of industries including iron smelting and steelmaking.

Shipbuilding, shipping and fishing are major features of the economies of Northern Europe. Sweden and Finland are leading shipbuilders and Norway has the world's eighth largest shipping fleet. More than three-quarters of Iceland's exports are fish products. In contrast, meat and dairy products are major Danish exports.

A river plunges over a waterfall in northern Norway

WESTERN EUROPE

Population: 314,201,000.
Area: 2,045,416 sq km (789,735 sq miles).
Population density: 153 per sq km (397 per sq mile).
Economy: The average gross national product per person in 1984 was $7,878, ranging from Switzerland's $16,000 to Portugal's $1,970.

Western Europe consists of 17 countries and includes some of the world's leading economic powers, such as West Germany (the world's fourth most important industrial nation), France, Britain and Italy. This comparatively small and densely populated region has had a tremendous influence on the rest of the world. In the Age of Exploration, which began in the 15th century, West Europeans traveled to all parts of the world, founding colonies and spreading Christianity. Today, many European languages are spoken around the world.

Ireland
Republic
Cap: Dublin
Pop: 3,624,000
Area: 70,300 sq km
(27,100 sq miles)

Great Britain
Monarchy
Cap: London
Pop: 56,500,000
Area: 165,300 sq km
(63,800 sq miles)

Belgium
Monarchy
Cap: Brussels
Pop: 9,868,000
Area: 30,500 sq km
(11,700 sq miles)

Netherlands
Monarchy
Cap: Amsterdam
Pop: 14,536,000
Area: 40,800 sq km
(15,750 sq miles)

Luxembourg
Monarchy
Cap: Luxembourg
Pop: 367,000
Area: 2,600 sq km
(1,000 sq miles)

Malta
Republic
Cap: Valletta
Pop: 354,000
Area: 316 sq km
(123 sq miles)

West Germany
Republic
Cap: Bonn
Pop: 60,700,000
Area: 248,600 sq km
(96,000 sq miles)

Portugal
Republic
Cap: Lisbon
Pop: 10,095,000
Area: 92,100 sq km
(35,500 sq miles)

Switzerland
Republic
Cap: Bern
Pop: 6,466,000
Area: 41,200 sq km
(16,000 sq miles)

Spain
Monarchy
Cap: Madrid
Pop: 39,075,000
Area: 504,800 sq km
(194,800 sq miles)

Italy
Republic
Cap: Rome
Pop: 57,226,000
Area: 301,200 sq km
(116,250 sq miles)

Andorra
Principality
Cap: Andorra la Vella
Pop: 49,000
Area: 450 sq km
(175 sq miles)

France
Republic
Cap: Paris
Pop: 55,239,000
Area: 547,000 sq km
(211,150 sq miles)

Monaco
Monarchy
Cap: Monaco
Pop: 28,000
Area: 1.9 sq km
(0.73 sq miles)

Liechtenstein
Principality
Cap: Vaduz
Pop: 28,000
Area: 157 sq km
(61 sq miles)

San Marino
Republic
Cap: San Marino
Pop: 23,000
Area: 61 sq km
(23.5 sq miles)

Land and climate

Western Europe has three distinct types of climate. In the northwestern parts – affected by moist southwesterly winds from the Atlantic Ocean – the "maritime" climate is predominantly cool and wet. But the Gulf Stream, a warm ocean current which flows across the Atlantic from the Gulf of Mexico, maintains winter temperatures. The southern part of Western Europe has hot, dry summers and mild, moist winters. This is the characteristic "Mediterranean" climate. Central and eastern parts have "continental" climates which become increasingly extreme the further the countries are from the sea. Summers are hot but winters are bitterly cold.

The landscape of Western Europe has two distinct features. One is the broad, fertile North European Plain that extends from southeastern England, across northwest France, the Low Countries (The Netherlands, Belgium and Luxembourg), Germany and Poland, into the USSR. The other is the band of uplands that runs through central and southern Europe. Much of it is more hilly than mountainous, but it does include the major, and comparatively recently formed, mountain ranges of the Pyrenees and the Alps.

Rain is common in England's maritime climate

Dutch windmills once drained the land

The Mediterranean climate of Majorca

Art and culture

The art and culture of Western Europe has had a profound influence on the rest of the world. The cultural tradition can be traced from Ancient Greece, but its characteristic qualities were really established in Italy during the Roman Empire. Although the tradition declined during the Middle Ages, it was recreated in Italy during the 15th-century revival of classical scholarship and art called the Renaissance. This period produced many of the world's finest painters, sculptors and architects.

Other civilizations have influenced European culture, however. For example, the Moors, Muslims from North Africa who occupied Spain for 700 years, left behind many wonderful examples of Islamic architecture. The culture of Western Europe is still influenced today by people of African or Asian origin from former colonies who have settled in

Heidelberg is a famous German university city

Europe, following the decline of the European Empires between the late 1940s and the 1970s. All that remains of the British Empire, formerly the world's largest, are a few small, scattered territories, including Gibraltar.

The literature of Western Europe has had a remarkable impact on the culture of the West because of the spread of European languages – especially English, French, German and Spanish. Writers, such as Cervantes, Dickens, Goethe, Molière, Shakespeare and Schiller, are known throughout the world. Classical music also has its roots firmly set in Europe, and the works of German and North Italian composers, such as Bach, Beethoven, Wagner, Puccini and Verdi, are performed worldwide.

Botticelli's *Primavera* hangs in the Uffizi Gallery, Florence

Ways of life

Much of Western Europe lay in ruins in 1945, at the end of World War II. Nevertheless, many countries recovered quickly, with aid from the United States. West Germany, for example, achieved such remarkable progress in all economic areas and ways of life that its post-war revival is sometimes referred to as an "economic miracle." Economic growth in most of Europe was high in the 1950s and 1960s. In the 1970s, however, a world recession and high inflation rates hit most of the industrialized nations.

All the larger countries in Western Europe are democracies, within broadly capitalist, free-market economies. Economic recession in the 1970s and the changing nature of industry have caused unemployment and

Real growth	USA	JAPAN	WEST GERMANY	UNITED KINGDOM
1960	2.1	13.1	8.9	4.9
1965	6.0	5.1	5.6	2.1
1970	−0.1	9.4	5.1	2.3
1975	−1.0	2.6	−1.6	−0.6
1980	0	4.4	1.4	−2.3
1985	3.0	4.5	2.6	3.7
1986	2.5	2.6	2.4	2.9
Inflation rate				
1960	1.6	3.6	1.4	1.0
1965	1.7	6.6	3.4	4.8
1970	5.9	7.7	3.4	6.4
1975	9.1	11.8	6.0	24.2
1980	13.5	8.0	5.5	18.0
1985	3.5	2.1	2.5	6.1
1986	2.0	0.4	−0.2	3.4

Figures represent percentage change from previous year

A woman buys vegetables at a street market in Italy

political unrest, however. Most governments have used strict economic policies to reduce inflation and stabilize the prices of essentials such as food and fuel.

In recent years ways of life in Western Europe have become ever more similar, particularly in the cities, where most of the populations live. The majority of Western European families live in apartments or small houses, have regular employment for about forty hours a week, pay taxes, enjoy mostly free health care provided by national insurance schemes, and benefit from free education.

Almost every country in Western Europe has its own military force, and some have compulsory military service. Switzerland, a neutral country, has no permanent army but provides regular, compulsory periods of combat training for its population.

National identity

Until the end of World War II in 1945, Western European nations were deeply divided and rivalries led to some of the world's most destructive wars. One of the results of these wars was the loss of territories by the defeated countries as peace terms were settled. People who had spent their lives in one country were suddenly absorbed into another.

Since 1945, however, attempts have been made to increase cooperation and thus create stability. But many differences of language and religion remain. For example, Belgium has two rival groups of people: the Dutch-speaking Flemings and the French-speaking Walloons. In Spain some Basques want to form their own country.

Spanish musicians in traditional dress

Religion

Swiss Guards outside the Pope's residence, Vatican City

In Western Europe as a whole the majority of Christians are members of the Roman Catholic Church. They are concentrated in the southern parts of the region, however. By contrast, the more northern countries, such as Britain and West Germany, contain more Protestants. Protestant Christian beliefs derive from a theological rebellion against Roman Catholicism in the 16th century. Lutherans, Calvinists, Methodists, Presbyterians and Anglicans are all Protestants. In many countries the Church supports or runs schools, and in Spain, for instance, it has greatly influenced the educational system. The Roman Catholic Church has also had a profound effect on Western culture.

Recent history

Western European nations have founded several organizations to encourage cooperation and prevent conflict of the type that led to two World Wars. The best known is the European Economic Community (EEC), which was founded by West Germany, Italy, Belgium, France, Luxembourg and the Netherlands. These six have now been joined by Denmark, Greece, Ireland, Portugal, Spain and Britain. Economic cooperation is not always easy. Some farmers, notably in France, have objected to imports of farm products that are cheaper than those they produce themselves. Some leaders of the EEC want to turn the organization into a political union – a United States of Europe – others want to retain their own national identities.

Most West European nations feel threatened by the USSR and its allies in Eastern Europe. They have joined together, with the United States, to form a defence alliance – the North Atlantic Trea-

Rioters burn a car in a Northern Ireland street

ty Organization (NATO). But conflict still continues in some areas, such as Northern Ireland, where the people are divided by religion. Many Irish Roman Catholics would like Northern Ireland to be reunited with the Republic of Ireland. But most Protestants, who form the majority, want the region to remain British. Both the British and the Irish governments have sought unsuccessfully to find a solution to this difficult problem.

French students demonstrate

French farmers block the road against foreign imports

Economy

Western Europe is rich in mineral resources, including coal, oil, natural gas and iron ore, and is the most heavily industrialized region of the world. It was in Britain that the Industrial Revolution began in the late 1700s. Since then, industry has replaced agriculture in economic importance.

Most electricity for industry is generated by coal, oil and natural gas, although in mountainous countries, such as Switzerland, hydroelectric power is of great importance. Nuclear energy is also important in several countries, including France and Britain, although some people regard nuclear power stations as threats to the environment.

Major crops in Western Europe include grapes (for wine-making), olives, potatoes, sugarbeet, vegetables, barley and wheat. Livestock farming is also important. Many farms are highly mechanized and efficient (in Britain farming employs only 3 per cent of the workforce). European farming methods, such as Dutch land reclamation techniques, have been widely copied. Today, about two-fifths of the Netherlands is below sea level at high tide

West Germany is the most economically powerful nation of the group, and is one of the world's major producers of iron and steel, chemicals and machinery. It has good resources of iron, coal and potash, but has to import oil, aluminum ore (bauxite) and other nonferrous metals.

Grapes for wine-making being tested in Portugal

Dutch land reclamation

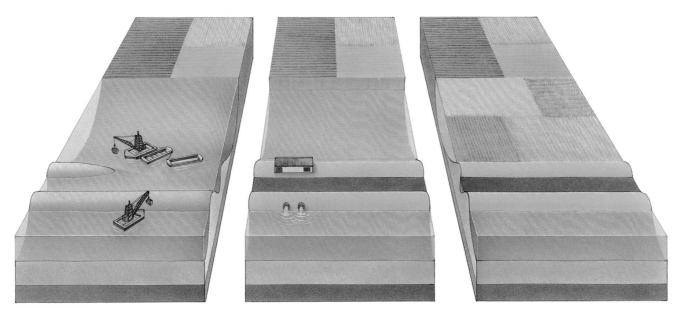

Dykes are built with clay and sand to keep out sea

Pumphouse removes water gradually to dry out land

In 10-15 years the reclaimed land is suitable for cultivation

Many people have moved from country areas to settle in the cities. Until recently, most of them found jobs in manufacturing industries, such as steelmaking, shipbuilding, car manufacture and mining. But today the decline of traditional industries, and their replacement by high-technology ones, which require only small workforces, has meant that an increasing number of people work in service industries, including tourism. In several countries, such as France, Italy, Portugal and Spain, tourism is a major source of foreign earnings. Other important service industries, such as banking and insurance, are concerned with international finance, and Switzerland is one of the chief banking centers of the world.

High technology car manufacture in Turin, Italy

A huge excavator extracts lignite (brown coal) in West Germany

CENTRAL/EASTERN EUROPE

Central and Eastern Europe contain ten countries, all of which – except Austria and Greece – are Communist countries. Six of the eight Communist nations – East Germany, Poland, Czechoslovakia, Hungary, Rumania and Bulgaria – are directly allied to the USSR. Eastern Europe includes the poorest nation in Europe, Albania. As in Western Europe, the people of Central and Eastern Europe worked hard from 1945 to rebuild their devastated countries. They created many new industries but today their standards of living are much lower than those of their western neighbors.

East Germany
Republic
Cap: East Berlin
Pop: 16,700,000
Area: 108,200 sq km
(41,750 sq miles)

Czechoslovakia
Republic
Cap: Prague
Pop: 15,500,000
Area: 127,900 sq km
(49,350 sq miles)

Austria
Republic
Cap: Vienna
Pop: 7,550,000
Area: 84,800 sq km
(32,350 sq miles)

Yugoslavia
Republic
Cap: Belgrade
Pop: 23,284,000
Area: 255,800 sq km
(98,750 sq miles)

Greece
Republic
Cap: Athens
Pop: 9,954,000
Area: 132,000 sq km
(51,000 sq miles)

Albania
Republic
Cap: Tiranë
Pop: 3,000,000
Area: 28,750 sq km
(11,100 sq miles)

Bulgaria
Republic
Cap: Sofia
Pop: 8,990,000
Area: 110,900 sq km
(42,800 sq miles)

Poland
Republic
Cap: Warsaw
Pop: 37,550,000
Area: 312,700 sq km
(120,700 sq miles)

Hungary
Republic
Cap: Budapest
Pop: 10,600,000
Area: 93,000 sq km
(35,900 sq miles)

Rumania
Republic
Cap: Bucharest
Pop: 22,800,000
Area: 237,500 sq km
(91,650 sq miles)

EAST GERMANY
POLAND
CZECHOSLOVAKIA
AUSTRIA
HUNGARY
RUMANIA
YUGOSLAVIA
BULGARIA
ALBANIA
GREECE

Land and climate

The landscape of Central and Eastern Europe varies dramatically from north to south. In the north, the North German Plain broadens as it stretches eastward, giving the greater part of East Germany and almost all of Poland some of the best agricultural land in Europe. To the south lie the highlands of Czechoslovakia, the Carpathian Mountains (an extension of the Alpine mountain system) and the Transylvanian Alps. The Balkan peninsula, which includes Albania, Greece, much of Bulgaria and most of Yugoslavia, is a largely rugged upland. But the region does include lowlands in the wide valley of the Danube River and the flat Hungarian Plain.

These lowlands extend eastward toward the Black Sea, through southern Rumania and northern Bulgaria. They are broken only by the Transylvanian Alps, which divide Rumania and link the Carpathian and Balkan mountain ranges.

The climate of Central and Eastern Europe varies from the cold Northern European climate of northern Poland and East Germany to the Mediterranean climate found in coastal Yugoslavia, Albania and Greece. Between these extremes, most of the region has a "continental moist" climate, with warm summers, cool winters, and rainfall all the year round.

The Danube River flows through Budapest

The River Danube

Greece's Mediterranean climate is well-suited to fishermen

Ways of life

In Austria most of the population lives in urban areas, with 20 per cent living in the capital, Vienna. Although relatively few Austrians work in agriculture, Austria is nevertheless self-sufficient in many food products as a result of intensive, mechanized farming. In contrast, approximately half the populations of Albania, Hungary, Bulgaria and Rumania live and work in rural areas, making their living from farming. East Germany was formerly a mainly agricultural region, but it is now one of the world's top ten industrial powers. Yugoslavia, although communist, has received aid from Western Europe. Despite high inflation it has new industries, and many workers now live in urban areas.

New apartment blocks in Belgrade, Yugoslavia

Language

Apart from Hungarian, the languages spoken in Central and Eastern Europe belong to the Indo-European language family. Most of them are part of the Balto-Slavic group within that family. Exceptions are the languages of Albania and Greece, which belong to a group of their own; East Germany and Austria, where people speak German; and Rumania, where the language belongs to the Romance group, like French and Italian, a consequence of ancient Roman occupation. The Hungarian language belongs to the Uralic-Altaic group, like Finnish. Two alphabets are used: Cyrillic and Roman. In Yugoslavia, the Serbs and the Croats both speak Serbo-Croatian but the Serbs write it in Cyrillic whereas the Croats use the Roman alphabet.

English alphabet

ABCDEFGHIJKLMNOPQRSTUVWXYZ

Greek alphabet

ΑΒΓΔΕΖΗΘΙΚΛΜΝΞΟΠΡΣΤΥΦΧΨΩ

Russian alphabet

АБВГДЕЁЖЗИКЛМНОПРСТУФХЦЧШЩЪ
ЫЬЭЮЯ

Culture

Historically the greatest contribution made by any country to Western culture came from Greece. More than 2,000 years ago Greek artists and scholars laid foundations for architecture, drama, poetry and sculpture that still form the basis of many of our cultural and artistic values.

Much of the richness of 19th- and early 20th-century European culture originated in Central Europe. This is principally because the Austro-Hungarian Empire, with its cultural heart in Vienna, was such a powerful and effective patron of the arts. Music was particularly encouraged. Austrian composers such as Schubert, Strauss and Mozart became as well known as Bach and Beethoven from neighboring Germany. Other arts flourished too, especially in the early years of this century. Artists, such as Gustav Klimt and Egon Schiele, worked in Vienna, and influential movements in the decorative arts and architecture, such as Art Nouveau, developed there also. Other Central and Eastern European countries have also produced fine musicians, such as Dvořák (Czech), Liszt and Bartók (Hungarian) and Chopin (Polish).

The Acropolis is a legacy of Greek civilisation

Religion

In the Communist nations, the practice of any form of religion is discouraged and Albania is officially atheist. Nevertheless many people continue to hold religious beliefs. The great majority of Christians are either Eastern Orthodox or Roman Catholic; a smaller proportion are Protestant. There are also Muslims in Albania, Bulgaria and Yugoslavia.

Polish people going to church on Palm Sunday

Communism

Communism is the official political, economic and social doctrine in Albania, Bulgaria, Czechoslovakia, East Germany, Hungary, Poland, Rumania and Yugoslavia. The dominant influence in the area is the USSR. Soviet policies do not officially control their European allies, but nevertheless they strongly influence the Communist governments of all but Albania and Yugoslavia.

A statue of Lenin, father of Communism

A city divided

Before World War II, Berlin was the capital of all Germany. After Germany's defeat in 1945, Berlin became located within East Germany and the victorious Allied Forces (Britain, France, the United States and the USSR) divided the city into four sections, and each took responsibility for policing its own zone. Relations between the USSR and the West worsened during the Cold War in the 1950s. Finally, in 1961, East Germany (influenced by the USSR) built a wall 42 km (26 miles) long through the city. The Berlin Wall divides the city into western and eastern zones (belonging to West and East Germany), prevents unauthorized travel between east and west, and leaves West Berlin isolated within East Germany. West Berlin has become an outpost of the West in which West Berliners and its visitors from elsewhere in Western Europe enjoy a lifestyle that is in marked contrast to that of their Communist neighbors on the other side of the Wall.

The Berlin Wall divides East and West Berlin

Recent history

Central and Eastern Europe since World War II have been the principal focus of Soviet influence. The advance of Soviet troops in 1945 helped establish the present borders between Communist and non-Communist European countries. Since then deviations from Soviet influence have been crushed or controlled in Hungary (1956), Czechoslovakia (1968) and most recently in Poland, where the Solidarity movement, founded in 1980 but banned in 1982, opposed government policies.

Albania became a "client state" of the USSR in 1955. It severed its links in 1961 and has remained independent since. Yugoslavia was allied with the USSR after World War II but soon drifted away from Soviet influence.

Austria, a non-Communist country, has become prosperous with US aid. Greece suffered civil war from 1944 to 1950 and military dictatorship between 1967 and 1973 in the process of restoring democracy and rebuilding the economy.

Lech Walesa, founder of Solidarity

Soviet tanks in Prague, Czechoslovakia, in 1968

Economy

Industry in Central and Eastern Europe is based on the many natural resources found there, such as iron ore, coal, natural gas, bauxite (aluminum ore) and mercury. These resources allow such industries as construction, steel-making, machinery manufacture and chemicals to develop. East Germany, the region's leading industrial power, is one of the world's largest producers of iron and steel products. It is also a major producer of chemicals and precision instruments.

Forests are an important natural resource in the north and central parts of the region. These give rise to such industries as pulp- and paper-making. The countries in the region are also self-sufficient in nearly all their agricultural produce. An exception is Greece, which imports most of its livestock requirements.

In many of the Communist countries, industrial and agricultural operations are owned by the government, and not by individual people or companies, although many families have their own small plot of land and sell surplus produce privately.

In contrast to most Communist countries, most agricultural land in Poland is privately-owned by farmers

Farmland covers three-fifths of Poland. The Communist government introduced collective and state farms in an attempt to end private ownership. But Polish farmers opposed this policy and today about three-quarters of the land is privately owned.

The government's industrial policies were more successful and Poland is now one of the top 15 industrial powers. It makes many products, including ships in the northern, Baltic Sea ports, steel, chemicals, fertilizers, paper and many processed foods. Nearly 50 per cent of Poland's exports are machinery and equipment.

Gdansk is Poland's major ship-building city

SOVIET UNION

Population:
Total: 279,904,000.
European USSR:
211,308,000.
Asian USSR: 68,596,000.
Area:
Total: 22,402,200 sq km
(8,647,250 sq miles).
European USSR: 5,571,000
sq km (2,150,400 sq miles).
Asian USSR: 16,831,200 sq
km (6,496,800 sq miles).
Overall population density:
12 per sq km (4.6 per sq mile).
Economy: The gross national
product per person in 1984
was US $7,120.

The Union of Soviet Socialist Republics (USSR) is the world's largest country. It extends nearly a quarter of the way around the world from its border with Poland in the west to the Pacific Ocean in the east, a distance of more than 8,000 km (5,000 miles). The USSR occupies more than half of Europe and two-fifths of Asia, and in all covers nearly one-seventh of the world's total landmass.

Although the USSR has a central government in Moscow, it is in fact a federation of 15 republics. Overall political control lies in the hands of the Communist Party of the Soviet Union, which has more than 18 million party members and makes up approximately six per cent of the total population. Just over half the population are Russians. Approximately 15 per cent are Ukrainian; the remaining 35 per cent come from more than 100 other ethnic groups.

NORTHERN ASIA

S O V I E T   U N I O N

EUROPE

Soviet Union
Republic
Cap: Moscow
Pop: 279,900,000
Area: 22,402,200 sq km
(8,647,250 sq miles)

Land and climate

The USSR can be divided into six geographical regions. These are the European Plain, the low Ural Mountains, the Ural-Caspian Lowlands, the West Siberian Plain, the Central Siberian Plateau, and the Eastern Siberian Uplands.

The European Plain is mostly flat land about 180 m (600 ft) above sea level. The Ural-Caspian Lowlands have sandy deserts and low plateaux. The Western Siberian Plain is the largest flat area in the world. It covers more than 2.6 million sq km (1 million sq miles). Drainage is poor and the region is mostly marshland or forest. The Central Siberian Plateau stands about 610 meters (2,000 ft) above sea level. It is a cold region with coniferous forests (taiga) and treeless arctic plains (tundra). The wild Eastern Siberian Upland has rugged mountains and windswept plateaux.

Part of the USSR lies within the Arctic Circle and is renowned for its bitter winters. Snow covers half the country for six months of the year. Temperatures range between −46°C (−51°F) in winter and 16°C (61°F) in summer. The southern deserts, in contrast, have average summer temperatures of 32°C (90°F). The heaviest rainfall is in the Caucasus Mountains, which have 250 cm (100 inches) per year.

A tree-lined lake on the taiga in Siberia

Sheep graze among the rugged Caucasus Mountains

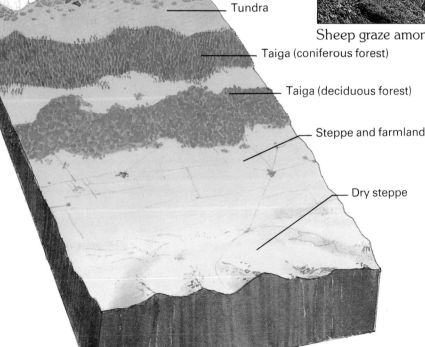

- Ice cap
- Tundra
- Taiga (coniferous forest)
- Taiga (deciduous forest)
- Steppe and farmland
- Dry steppe

The tundra extends from the ice cap in the north, south to the taiga. Treeless, and with permafrost all the year round, the tundra is a bleak arctic plain. From the coniferous forests of the taiga, which are often swampy, the treeless steppe begins. Here the land is drier, and suitable for some farmland. Further south the steppe gives way to rising uplands and mountains.

People and ways of life

The USSR is often called Russia, but Russia is really only one of the 15 republics that make up the USSR. The people of the USSR come from a wide variety of nationalities. About 53 per cent of the population is from the Russian nationality group, and Russian is the official language. After the Russian Revolution in 1917, the Communists turned many places of worship into museums or study centers. Nevertheless, large numbers of Russian Orthodox Christians, Muslims and Jews still practice their faiths and the government's official policy is to protect and preserve minority cultures. Following the terrible destruction of World War II, the Soviet government concentrated on building heavy industries, including armament plants, and neglected consumer industries.

Arab decoration on a Mosque in Samarkand, Uzbekistan

Soci is a holiday resort on the Black Sea

A Soviet woman van driver changes a tire

Over half of the population of the USSR live in cities. More than 20 Soviet cities have a population of more than 1 million people. The largest are Moscow, Leningrad, Kiev, Tashkent, Baku, Kharkov, Minsk, Gorki and Novosibirsk. About 1 million people a year move from rural to urban areas.

In the USSR, a large proportion – more than 50 per cent – of the female population work in paid employment. Children are looked after in government-run kindergartens. Women do every kind of work, even heavy manual labour; 75 per cent of Russia's doctors are women.

Russians are enthusiastic about sports and have achieved the highest standards in the Olympics and other world championships. The most popular sport is soccer. Chess is also popular, with many children learning to play well at an early age. Many famous chess masters are from USSR.

The USSR's World War II alliance with the Western Allies broke down after 1945. It was followed by a period of suspicion and hostility called the Cold War. In more recent years relations have improved between the USSR and the United States, the world's two superpowers. Nevertheless, tension has risen over the USSR's 1978 invasion of Afghanistan, and the build-up of nuclear weapons by both countries.

In space exploration the USSR took the lead initially with the successful launch of the first artificial satellite, *Sputnik*, in 1957, and the first manned orbit of the Earth by Yuri Gagarin in 1961. The USSR then fell behind as the United States developed the Apollo and Space Shuttle programs, but it is now trying to regain the lead.

The USSR has been less successful in other technological areas, and in making the best of its agriculture. Several poor harvests have forced the USSR to purchase huge quantities of grain from the United States and elsewhere. From the mid-1980s, under the leadership of Mikhail Gorbachev, attempts have been made to revitalize the economy, introduce more personal freedom and reopen negotiations on world disarmament.

A Soyuz spacecraft

Soviet leaders review a military parade in front of Lenin's tomb, Moscow

Economy

The USSR government has control over all industry; its agents tell the factories what to make and where to sell their products. Prices and wages are also fixed by the government.

Farmland covers one-third of the USSR, which has more farmland than any other country in the world. If the harvest is good, the USSR is self-sufficient. The USSR leads the world in producing barley, wheat, lamb, oats, potatoes and milk. The richest soils are those of the western USSR, however, and the nuclear accident at Chernobyl in 1986 threatened part of this region by polluting agricultural land with radioactive fallout. About 40 per cent of the country's farms are government-run. The rest are run by collectives made up of as many as 400 families.

The USSR has huge mineral resources, and leads the world in producing asbestos, coal, oil and natural gas, lead, manganese, nickel, potash and silver. Mining is one of the USSR's major industries. Tin is the only mineral it imports. Only about seven per cent of the USSR's electricity is produced by nuclear power.

Vladivostok, in the eastern USSR

The Trans-Siberian Railroad

Steel production is a key industry in the USSR

The majority of its electrical power is derived from burning fossil fuels (74 per cent), and 29 per cent is produced in hydroelectric stations. Natural gas is exported to the West or exchanged for technological assistance.

The USSR is the second largest producer of manufactured goods in the world. Manufactured products include steel, fertilizers, machinery, cars, tractors, chemicals, timber products and cement. Moscow is the country's leading manufacturing city.

Two-thirds of the USSR's freight traffic travels by rail. One line, the Trans-Siberian railway, runs from Moscow in the west to Vladivostok on the Pacific coast, covering 9,000 km (5,600 miles). The journey takes about seven days. Aeroflot, the national airline, is the world's largest government-owned airline.

Strip-mining

Farmland

Direction of mining

Topsoil

Overburden

Coal seam

Overburden fills last strip

Flax for making linen and linseed oil being harvested on a collective farm in Grodno, western USSR

ORGANIZATIONS

Many international organizations are based in Europe. Most are economic, several are linked to the United Nations, and two are military.

Economic organizations include the European Economic Community (EEC), based in Brussels; the European Free Trade Association (EFTA), based in Stockholm; the Council for Mutual Economic Aid (COMECON), based in Moscow; and the Organization for Economic Cooperation and Development (OECD), based in Paris. All seek to facilitate trade between member nations and protect them against competition from other sources.

The two European military and mutual defense organizations are the North Atlantic Treaty Organization (NATO), based in Brussels, and the Warsaw Pact, based in Moscow. Both offer any member nation the protection and support of the whole organization against armed attack, and provide a unified military command.

The United Nations has a European office and Secretariat in Geneva. Many associated agencies are also based in Europe.

American and European ships on a NATO exercise

BENELUX
Belgium
Luxembourg
Netherlands

COMECON
Bulgaria
Cuba
Czechoslovakia
East Germany
Hungary
Mongolia

Poland
Rumania
USSR

EEC
Belgium
France
Italy
Luxembourg
Netherlands
West Germany
Denmark

Ireland
UK
Greece
Spain
Portugal

EFTA
Austria
Finland
Iceland
Norway
* Portugal
special status

Sweden
Switzerland

NATO
Belgium
Canada
Denmark
France
Greece
Iceland
Italy
Luxembourg

Netherlands
Norway
Portugal
Turkey
UK
USA
West Germany

**NORDIC
COUNCIL**
Denmark
Finland

Iceland
Norway
Sweden

WARSAW PACT
Bulgaria
Czechoslovakia
East Germany
Hungary
Poland
Rumania
USSR

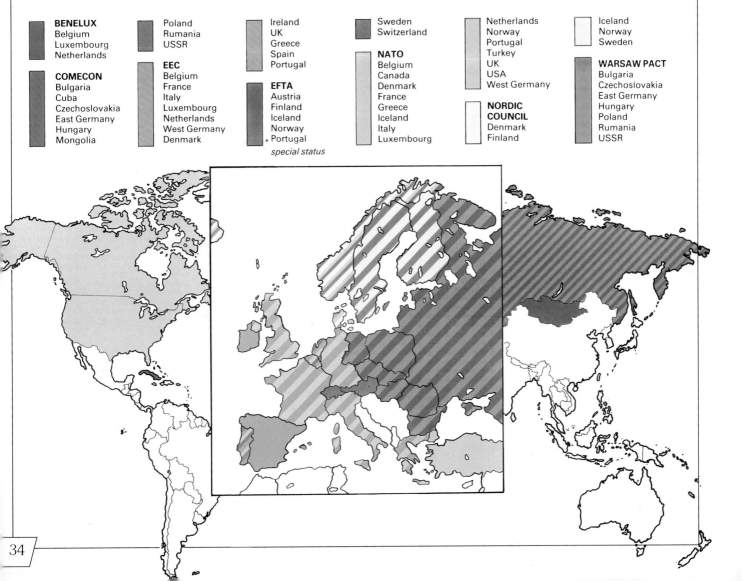

GLOSSARY

CLIMATE AND WEATHER

Maritime Climate Near to or bordering on the sea.
Mediterranean Climate Like that around the Mediterranean Sea – hot, dry summers and warm, wet winters.
Polar Climate Very cold, as in the Arctic or Antarctic.
Temperate Climate Lacking extremes of temperatures.

ECONOMIC SYSTEMS

Capitalist Individuals own the means of production, land, factories, etc. and employ other people to work for them to produce goods and services at a profit.
Communist The state (the 'people') owns and controls the means of production, in order to share more evenly the wealth created by their work.

ECONOMIC TERMS

Exports Goods sold outside the country in which they were produced.
Gross national product (GNP) The total value of all goods and services produced by a country (usually in a year).
Imports Goods from one country brought into another to be sold.
Industrialized Nation One which has well developed industry as an important part of its economy.
Inflation Sudden rise in prices caused by availability of too much money.
Manufactured goods Made from raw materials or individual components either by hand or by machines.
Mass production Manufacture of goods (often identical) in large quantities, often on a production line.
Resources Materials that meet a need, eg iron ore to make steel, or good soil for growing crops.

GEOGRAPHICAL TERMS

Coniferous forest Has cone-bearing trees (conifers).
Deciduous forest Has trees that lose their leaves in autumn.
Desert Region with little rainfall and few plants and animals; usually sandy. It may be either hot or cold.
Fiord Deep, narrow, steep-sided bay on the coast created by the action of glaciers.
Geyser Natural spring that spouts hot water into the air.
Glacier A mass or river of ice that forms in a high mountain valley and gradually carves its way downwards.
Geothermal power Electric power produced by harnessing the hot water of geysers.
Moraine accumulation of earth, stones and debris carried and deposited by glacier.
Peninsular Spur of land nearly surrounded by water.
Population density Average number of people living in a square kilometer (or mile), calculated by dividing the population of a country by its area.

Rural Based in the countryside rather than in the towns.
Steppe The vast treeless plains found in South Eastern Europe and Siberia below the arctic regions.
Strip-mining A mine that is worked from the surface once the overburden is removed, especially for coal. Also known as opencast mining.
Taiga Cold, swampy land with coniferous forest found for example, between the tundra and steppes of Siberia.
Temperate forest Grown in mild, rainy climates, usually broadleaved with trees that shed their leaves in winter.
Tundra Cold, treeless plain with little vegetation and wildlife, found in Arctic regions; the soil below the surface is permanently frozen.

RELIGIONS

Christianity Based on teachings of Jesus Christ and his followers. Practiced by Protestants, Roman Catholics etc.
Eastern Orthodox Eastern European branch of Catholic Church, without allegiances to Pope and Vatican.
Islam Based on the teachings of Mohammed, practised mainly among Arabs and Africans. Its followers are Muslims.
Judaism Based on the teachings of Moses. Its followers are called Jews.

TYPES OF GOVERNMENT AND POLITICAL TERMS

Colony Place settled by people who go to live there but who remain citizens of their place of birth.
Military government Sometimes unelected, supported by the force of the military.
Monarchy Government by a monarch (king or queen). In some, the power is limited, as in Britain or Sweden.
Republic Country in which the people elect the head of state and the government.

INDEX

All entries in bold are found in the Glossary

Photographic Credits:
Cover and pages 6 (both), 11 (right), 13 (both), 17 (bottom) and 18 (bottom): Hutchison Library; title page and page 10 (bottom): Tony Stone Assoc.; pages 5 (left), 9 (top), 13 (bottom), 21 (bottom), 23 (left), 25 (right), 29 (both), 30 (top and left) and 32 (right and bottom): Zefa; pages 5 (right), 7 (all), 10 (top), 12 (top), 15 (left), 16 (bottom), 18 (top), 20, 21 (top), 23 (right and bottom), 24, 25 (top and left), 26 (top) and 27 (both): Robert Harding; pages 9 (bottom), 12 (bottom), 15 (top and right) and 16 (top): Spectrum; page 11 (left): Photosource; pages 19 (top and left) and 26 (left and right): Frank Spooner Agency; pages 19 (right), 30 (right), 32 (left) and 33: Camera Press; pages 31 (both) and 34: The Research House.